"9Marks, as a ministry, has taken basic biblical teaching about the church and put it into the hands of pastors. Bobby, by way of these study guides, has taken this teaching and delivered it to the person in the pew. I am unaware of any other tool that so thoroughly and practically helps Christians understand God's plan for the local church. I can't wait to use these studies in my own congregation."

> **Jeramie Rinne,** Senior Pastor, South Shore Baptist Church, Hingham, Massachusetts

"Bobby Jamieson has done local church pastors an incredible service by writing these study guides. Clear, biblical, and practical, they introduce the biblical basis for a healthy church. But more importantly, they challenge and equip church members to be part of the process of improving their own church's health. The studies work for individual, small group, and larger group settings. I have used them for the last year at my own church and appreciate how easy they are to adapt to my own setting. I don't know of anything else like them. Highly recommended!"

> **Michael Lawrence,** Senior Pastor, Hinson Baptist Church, *Biblical Theology in the Life of the Church*

"This is a Bible study that is actually rooted in the Bible and involves actual study. In the 9Marks Healthy Church Study Guides series a new standard has been set for personal theological discovery and corresponding personal application. Rich exposition, compelling questions, and clear syntheses combine to give a guided tour of ecclesiology—the theology of the church. I know of no better curriculum for generating understanding of and involvement in the church than this. It will be a welcome resource in our church for years to come."

> **Rick Holland,** Senior Pastor, Mission Road Bible Church, Prairie Village, Kansas

"In America today we have the largest churches in the history of our nation, but the least amount of impact for Christ's kingdom. Slick marketing and finely polished vision statements are a foundation of sand. The 9Marks Healthy Church Study Guides series is a refreshing departure from church-growth materials, towards an in-depth study of God's Word that will equip God's people with his vision for his Church. These study guides will lead local congregations to abandon secular methodologies for church growth and instead rely on Christ's principles for developing healthy, God-honoring assemblies."

> **Carl J. Broggi,** Senior Pastor, Community Bible Church, Beaufort, South Carolina; President, Search the Scriptures Radio Ministry

"Anyone who loves Jesus will love what Jesus loves. The Bible clearly teaches that Jesus loves the church. He knows about and cares for individual churches and wants them to be spiritually healthy and vibrant. Not only has Jesus laid down his life for the church but he has also given many instructions in his Word regarding how churches are to live and function in the world. This series of Bible studies by 9Marks shows how Scripture teaches these things. Any Christian who works through this curriculum, preferably with other believers, will be helped to see in fresh ways the wisdom, love, and power of God in establishing the church on earth. These studies are biblical, practical, and accessible. I highly recommend this curriculum as a useful tool that will help any church embrace its calling to display the glory of God to a watching world."

> **Thomas Ascol,** Senior Pastor, Grace Baptist Church of Cape Coral, Florida; Executive Director, Founders Ministries

9MARKS HEALTHY CHURCH STUDY GUIDES

Built upon the Rock: The Church

Hearing God's Word: Expositional Preaching

The Whole Truth about God: Biblical Theology

God's Good News: The Gospel

Real Change: Conversion

Reaching the Lost: Evangelism

Committing to One Another: Church Membership

Guarding One Another: Church Discipline

Growing One Another: Discipleship in the Church

Leading One Another: Church Leadership

HEARING GOD'S WORD: EXPOSITIONAL PREACHING

Bobby Jamieson
Mark Dever, General Editor
Jonathan Leeman, Managing Editor

HEALTHY CHURCH STUDY GUIDES

Hearing God's Word: Expositional Preaching

Copyright © 2012 by 9Marks

Published by Crossway
1300 Crescent Street
Wheaton, Illinois 60187

Cover design: Dual Identity inc.

First printing 2012

Printed in the United States of America

Trade paperback ISBN: 978-1-4335-2528-5

PDF ISBN: 978-1-4335-2529-2

Mobipocket ISBN: 978-1-4335-2530-8

ePub ISBN: 978-1-4335-2531-5

Crossway is a publishing ministry of Good News Publishers.

VP		21	20	19	18	17	16	15	14	13	12
15	14	13	12	11	10	9	8	7	6	5	4	3	2

CONTENTS

INTRODUCTION

What does the local church mean to you?

Maybe you love your church. You love the people. You love the preaching and the singing. You can't wait to show up on Sunday, and you cherish fellowship with other church members throughout the week.

Then again, maybe your church is just a place you show up to a couple times a month. You sneak in late, duck out early.

We at 9Marks are convinced that the local church is where God means to display his glory to the nations. And we want to help you catch this vision, together with your whole church.

The 9Marks Healthy Church Study Guides are a series of six- or seven-week studies on each of the "nine marks of a healthy church" plus one introductory study. These nine marks are the core convictions of our ministry. To provide a quick introduction to them, we've included a chapter from Mark Dever's book *What Is a Healthy Church?* with each study. We don't claim that these nine marks are the most important things about the church or the only important things about the church. But we do believe that they are biblical and therefore helpful for churches.

So, in these studies, we're going to work through the biblical foundations and practical applications of each mark. The ten studies are:

- *Built upon the Rock: The Church* (the introductory study)
- *Hearing God's Word: Expositional Preaching*
- *The Whole Truth about God: Biblical Theology*
- *God's Good News: The Gospel*
- *Real Change: Conversion*
- *Reaching the Lost: Evangelism*
- *Committing to One Another: Church Membership*

- *Guarding One Another: Church Discipline*
- *Growing One Another: Discipleship in the Church*
- *Leading One Another: Church Leadership*

Each session of these studies takes a close look at one or more passages of Scripture and considers how to apply it to the life of your congregation. We hope they are equally appropriate for Sunday school, small groups, and other contexts where a group of two to two-hundred people can come together and discuss God's Word.

These studies are mainly driven by observation, interpretation, and application questions, so get ready to speak up! We also hope that these studies provide opportunities for people to reflect together on their experiences in the church, whatever those experiences may be.

"First things first," goes the old saying. If your house is on fire, you better put that out before you attend to a tea kettle that's starting to boil over.

What do you think is the first thing to attend to in a church?

We're convinced from Scripture that the matter of first importance in the church is preaching. But not just any preaching.

This study is going to focus on expositional preaching—preaching in which the main point of a biblical text becomes the main point of the sermon and is applied to life today. This is how pastors should preach. God calls pastors not to preach their own opinions or agendas; he calls them to preach his Word.

Expositional preaching is what gives life and health to the church. It's what shapes, forms, and reforms the church. It reveals God to us. It confronts our sin. It comforts us. It brings us to Christ. And it teaches us how to live together in a way that puts God's glorious character on display for all the world to see.

So let's jump into these six sessions and talk about:

- Why we need to hear God's Word
- Why the church should be fed by expositional preaching
- How expositional preaching works
- How we all should minister the Word to each other
- And more

AN ESSENTIAL MARK OF A HEALTHY CHURCH: EXPOSITIONAL PREACHING

BY MARK DEVER

(Originally published as chapter 5 of What Is a Healthy Church?*)*

If a healthy church is a congregation that increasingly displays the character of God as his character has been revealed in his Word, the most obvious place to begin building a healthy church is to call Christians to listen to God's Word. God's Word is the source of all life and health. It's what feeds, develops, and preserves a church's understanding of the gospel itself.

WHAT IT IS

Fundamentally, this means that both pastors and congregations must be committed to expositional preaching. Expositional preaching is the kind of preaching that, quite simply, exposes God's Word. It takes a particular passage of Scripture, explains that passage, and then applies the meaning of the passage to the life of the congregation. It's the kind of preaching most geared to get at what God says to his people, as well as to those who are not his people. A commitment to expositional preaching is a commitment to hear God's Word.

There are many other types of preaching. Topical preaching, for example, gathers up one or more Scriptures on a particular topic, such as the topic of prayer or the topic of giving. Biographical preaching takes the life of someone in the Bible and portrays the individual's life as a display of God's grace and as an example of hope and faithfulness. And these other types may be employed helpfully on occasion. But the regular diet of the church should consist of the explanation and application of particular portions of God's Word.

The practice of expositional preaching presumes a belief that what God says is authoritative for his people. It presumes that his people should hear it and need to hear it, lest our congregations be deprived of what God intends to use for shaping us after his image. It presumes that God intends the church to learn from both Testaments, as well as from every genre of Scripture—Law, History, Wisdom, Prophesy, Gospels, and Epistles. An expositional preacher who moves straight through books of the Bible and who regularly rotates between the different Testaments and genres of Scripture, I believe, is like a mother who serves her children food from every food group, not just their two or three favorite meals.

An expositional preacher's authority begins and ends with Scripture. Even as Old Testament prophets and New Testament apostles were given not just a commission to go and speak but also to speak a particular message, so Christian preachers today have authority to speak from God so long as they speak his words.

WHAT IT ISN'T

Someone may happily profess that God's Word is authoritative and that the Bible is inerrant. Yet if that person in practice (intentionally or not) does not preach expositionally, he denies his own claim.

Sometimes people confuse expositional preaching with the style of a particular expositional preacher whom they have observed. But expositional preaching is not fundamentally a matter of style. As others have observed, expositional preaching is not so much about how a preacher says what he says but about how a preacher decides what to say. Is Scripture determining our content or is something else? Expositional preaching is not marked by a particular form or style. Styles will vary. Instead it's marked by a biblical content.

Sometimes people confuse expositional preaching with reading a verse and then preaching on a topic loosely related to that verse. Yet when a preacher exhorts a congregation on a topic of his choosing, using biblical texts only to back up his point, he will never preach more than what he already knows. And the congregation will only learn what the preacher already knows. Expositional preaching requires more than that. It requires careful attention to the context of a passage because it aims to make the point of the biblical text the point of the sermon. When a preacher exhorts a congregation by preaching a passage of Scripture in context—where the point of the passage is the point of his sermon—both he and the congregation will end up hearing things from God that the preacher did not intend to say when he first sat down to study and prepare for the sermon. ("Next week, we'll look at Luke 1 and whatever God has for us in Luke 1. The following week, we'll look at Luke 2 and whatever God has for us in Luke 2. The week after that. . . .")

This should make sense as we think about every step of our Christian lives, from our initial call to repentance all the way to the Spirit's most recent work of conviction. Has not every step of growth in grace occurred when we heard from God in ways we hadn't heard from him before?

A preacher's ministry must be characterized by this very practical form of submission to the Word of God. Yet make no mistake: it is finally the congregation's responsibility to ensure that this is true of its preachers. Jesus assumes that congregations have the final responsibility for what happens in a church in Matthew 18 as does Paul in Galatians 1. A church, therefore, must never give a person spiritual oversight over the body who does not show a practical commitment to hearing and teaching God's Word. When it does, it hampers its growth, ensuring that it won't mature beyond the level of the pastor. The church will slowly be conformed to the image of the pastor rather than to the image of God.

THE WAY GOD HAS ALWAYS WORKED

God's people have always been created by God's Word. From creation in Genesis 1 to the call of Abram in Genesis 12, from the vision of the valley of the dry bones in Ezekiel 37 to the coming of the living Word, Jesus Christ—God has always created his people by his Word. As Paul wrote to the Romans, "Faith comes from hearing the message, and the message is heard through the word of Christ"

(Rom. 10:17 NIV). Or, as he wrote to the Corinthians, "Since in the wisdom of God the world through its wisdom did not know him, God was pleased through the foolishness of what was preached to save those who believe" (1 Cor. 1:21 NIV).

Sound, expositional preaching is often the fountainhead of true growth in a church. Martin Luther found that carefully attending to God's Word began the Reformation. We, too, must commit to seeing that our churches are always being reformed by the Word of God.

BACK TO THE HEART OF WORSHIP
During a day-long seminar on Puritanism that I taught at a church in London, I remarked at one point that Puritan sermons were sometimes two hours long. A member of the class gasped audibly and asked, "What time did that leave for worship?" Clearly, the individual assumed that listening to God's Word preached did not constitute worship. I replied that many English Protestants in former centuries believed that the most essential part of their worship was hearing God's Word in their own language (a freedom purchased by the blood of more than one martyr) and responding to it in their lives. Whether they had time to sing, though not entirely insignificant, was of comparatively little concern to them.

Our churches, too, must recover the centrality of the Word in our worship. Music is a biblically required response to God's Word, but the music God gave us was not given to build our churches upon. A church built on music—of whatever style—is a church built on shifting sands.

Christian, pray for your pastor—that he will commit himself to study Scripture rigorously, carefully, and earnestly. Pray that God will lead him to understand the Word, to apply it to his own life, and to apply it wisely to the church's life (see Luke 24:27; Acts 6:4; Eph. 6:19–20). Also, grant your pastor time during the week to prepare good sermons. Preaching is the fundamental component of pastoring. Then speak words of encouragement to him by telling him how the faithfulness he has shown to the Word has grown you in God's grace.

Pastor, pray these things for yourself. Pray also for other

churches in your neighborhood, city, nation, and around the world that preach and teach God's Word. Finally, pray that our churches would commit to hearing God's Word preached expositionally, so that the agenda of each church will be increasingly shaped by God's agenda in Scripture. Commitment to expositional preaching is an essential mark of a healthy church.

WEEK 1
WHAT IS TRUE
SPIRITUALITY?

GETTING STARTED

This entire six-week course is about expositional preaching:

- What it is
- Its biblical basis
- How it builds the church
- Why it's important for every church member to pay close attention to both what is preached and how it's preached

What Is Expositional Preaching?

Simply stated, expositional preaching is preaching that takes the main point of a text of Scripture, makes that the main point of the sermon, and applies it to life today. Expositional preaching is preaching that *exposes* the meaning of Scripture and brings it to bear on our lives.

Since the goal of expositional preaching is simply to explain and apply God's Word, we're going to take a step back for this first study and think about why God's Word is so important for the life and health of the church.

What Is True Spirituality?

In this first study we are going to consider the question, What is true spirituality? That's a question on a lot of people's minds today, not just Christians. While being "religious" is decidedly unpopular, spirituality is in, big-time.

1. What are some things you've heard non-Christians say about spirituality?

2. What are some things you've heard Christians say that true spirituality consists of?

MAIN IDEA

True spirituality consists in hearing, believing, and obeying God's Word. That is why God's Word is the source of the church's life and health, and why pastors should preach expositionally.

DIGGING IN

In Psalm 19 David writes,

[1] The heavens declare the glory of God,
    and the sky above proclaims his handiwork.
[2] Day to day pours out speech,
    and night to night reveals knowledge.
[3] There is no speech, nor are there words,
    whose voice is not heard.
[4] Their voice goes out through all the earth,
    and their words to the end of the world.
In them he has set a tent for the sun,
    [5] which comes out like a bridegroom leaving his chamber,
    and, like a strong man, runs its course with joy.
[6] Its rising is from the end of the heavens,
    and its circuit to the end of them,
    and there is nothing hidden from its heat.

[7] The law of the LORD is perfect,
    reviving the soul;
the testimony of the LORD is sure,
    making wise the simple;
[8] the precepts of the LORD are right,
    rejoicing the heart;
the commandment of the LORD is pure,
    enlightening the eyes;
[9] the fear of the LORD is clean,
    enduring forever;
the rules of the LORD are true,
    and righteous altogether.
[10] More to be desired are they than gold,
    even much fine gold;

sweeter also than honey
and drippings of the honeycomb.
[11] Moreover, by them is your servant warned;
in keeping them there is great reward.

[12] Who can discern his errors?
Declare me innocent from hidden faults.
[13] Keep back your servant also from presumptuous sins;
let them not have dominion over me!
Then I shall be blameless,
and innocent of great transgression.

[14] Let the words of my mouth and the meditation of my heart
be acceptable in your sight,
O LORD, my rock and my redeemer.

1. Verses 1 through 6 focus on one way God makes himself known and verses 7 through 11 focus on another. How would you summarize the two ways God reveals himself that are celebrated in this psalm?

2. What do we learn about God from his revelation of himself in creation (vv. 1–6)?

3. What can't the creation teach us about God and about how we are to relate to him?

4. What do the terms law (v. 7), testimony (v. 7), precepts (v. 8), commandment (v. 8), and rules (v. 9) all refer to? What does this suggest about how God communicates to us?

5. List all the things David says God's Word does in verses 7 through 11. Describe the human need or situation each of these actions addresses.

6. Based on this passage, how would you respond to someone who said that true spirituality is too deep for words?

Another passage that demonstrates the absolute centrality of God's Word in the Christian life is the familiar story of Mary and Martha from Luke 10:38–42:

[38] Now as they went on their way, Jesus entered a village. And a woman named Martha welcomed him into her house. [39] And she had a sister called Mary, who sat at the Lord's feet and listened to his teaching. [40] But Martha was distracted with much serving. And she went up to him and said, "Lord, do you not care that my sister has left me to serve alone? Tell her then to help me." [41] But the Lord answered her, "Martha, Martha, you are anxious and troubled about many things, [42] but one thing is necessary. Mary has chosen the good portion, which will not be taken away from her."

7. Describe Martha's activity and mind-set that we see in this passage.

8. Suppose we didn't have Jesus's words in verses 41–42, and you wanted to defend Martha. How might you make a case for why she is more spiritual than Mary?

9. What does Jesus commend Mary for doing? (Hint: It's not for simply giving herself a break!)

10. What does Jesus mean when he says that listening to his teaching is the "one thing" that is necessary?

A Spirituality of the Word

These two passages teach us that hearing, believing, and obeying God's Word is absolutely central to how we relate to God.

The New Testament teaches that we're born again through the Word of God (1 Pet. 1:23). We obtain faith through the Word of God (Rom. 10:17). We grow in godliness through the Word of God (John 17:17). And we receive encouragement and hope from the Word of God (Rom. 15:4).

These are some of the reasons why God's Word is the source and substance of true spirituality. True spirituality is a spirituality of the Word.

Why Pastors Should Preach Expositionally

Because God's Word is the source and substance of true spirituality, pastors should preach sermons in which the main point of the text of Scripture is the main point of the sermon. Expositional preaching is the starting point for a healthy church: God's Word teaches us who he is, how we have sinned against him, what he has done for us in Christ, what he requires of us in response, and how he provides everything we need—through his Word!—to bring him glory.

11. In light of the two passages we've studied, how would you respond to someone who said that in order to be really spiritual we need to:

  a) Contemplate images and icons that represent God?
  b) Pursue a direct, unmediated, mystical experience of the presence of God?
  c) Devote ourselves to social action, and discover God "at work" among the poor?
  d) Hear God speaking to us inwardly?

12. How should this understanding of Word-centered spirituality shape:

  a) What our churches do in their corporate gatherings?
  b) How we evaluate sermons?
  c) What we hope to get out of sermons?
  d) How we listen to sermons?

WEEK 2
WHY YOU ARE RESPONSIBLE FOR YOUR CHURCH'S TEACHING!

GETTING STARTED

1. *Have you ever walked out of a movie? Why?*

2. *When was the last time you changed the TV channel or radio station because you objected to the content? What would have been the effects of continuing to watch or listen?*

The reason many of us have walked out of movies, turned off TV shows, or changed the radio station is that we understand that we are responsible for what we see and hear. We must carefully weigh what we take in through media, what we allow to influence us, and what we approve of. This will sometimes mean rejecting what we see or hear by turning it off.

In a similar fashion, Scripture teaches that all Christians have a responsibility to ensure that the teaching they receive in their local churches is faithful to God's Word.

MAIN IDEA

Every church member is responsible for ensuring that the teaching in his or her church is faithful to God's Word.

DIGGING IN

One passage that teaches this clearly is Galatians 1. Paul begins his letter to the Galatians:

¹ Paul, an apostle—not from men nor through man, but through Jesus Christ and God the Father, who raised him from the dead— ² and all the brothers who are with me,

To the churches of Galatia:

³ Grace to you and peace from God our Father and the Lord Jesus Christ, ⁴ who gave himself for our sins to deliver us from the present evil age, according to the will of our God and Father, ⁵ to whom be the glory forever and ever. Amen.

⁶ I am astonished that you are so quickly deserting him who called you in the grace of Christ and are turning to a different gospel—⁷ not that there is another one, but there are some who trouble you and want to distort the gospel of Christ. ⁸ But even if we or an angel from heaven should preach to you a gospel contrary to the one we preached to you, let him be accursed. ⁹ As we have said before, so now I say again: If anyone is preaching to you a gospel contrary to the one you received, let him be accursed.

¹⁰ For am I now seeking the approval of man, or of God? Or am I trying to please man? If I were still trying to please man, I would not be a servant of Christ. (1:1–10)

1. *To whom does Paul address his letter (v. 2)? What implications does this have for how we read this passage?*

2. *What is Paul astonished about (v. 6)?*

3. *Describe the "some" Paul refers to in verse 7. Judging from the following verses, what are they doing to the Galatians?*

4. *Whom are the Galatians deserting (v. 6)? What does this tell us about the consequences of hearing and embracing false teaching?*

5. *On whom does Paul pronounce a curse (twice!) in verses 8 and 9? What does this teach us about Paul's understanding of the gospel?*

6. *Look back at verse 1. From whom does Paul derive his authority? Does this mean that everything Paul says is automatically true (see v. 8)?*

7. What does this say about the authority of pastors and elders today—where does it come from? How is that both similar to and different from Paul's authority?

Because the authority of a pastor's teaching is derived from and subject to God's Word, pastors should make it their aim to faithfully proclaim God's Word.

How should they do this? Generally speaking, pastors should preach through books of the Bible, making sure that the main point of the passage is the main point of the sermon. That way, God's Word sets the agenda for what a congregation learns, not the preacher.

8. Drawing on the whole passage, summarize in your own words what's wrong with the churches in Galatia and whom Paul holds responsible for this situation. (Hint: There may be more than one responsible party.)

9. Based on Paul's teaching in this passage, who would you say is responsible for what is taught in your local church?

10. What are some of the dangers of congregations entrusting this responsibility entirely to their leaders? In other words, what problems might arise if regular church members aren't exercising doctrinal discernment?

11. What does exercising this responsibility look like in practical terms for the average church member? What are some ways that the members of your church exercise responsibility for what is taught?

12. Does this mean congregations should begin to tell pastors what to preach? Or to appoint review committees for a pastor's sermons? How does a church simultaneously embrace this responsibility while also submitting to their leaders (Heb. 13:17)?

13. What are some ways you personally have exercised responsibility for what is taught? Are there more ways you can or should do this?

WEEK 3
THE POINT OF PREACHING —
WHAT MAKES A GOOD
SERMON GOOD?

GETTING STARTED

1. What's the purpose of listening to sermons?

2. What's not the purpose of listening to sermons? List several examples.

Two studies ago, we considered the fact that God grows and gives life to his people through his Word. And in the previous study, we saw in Galatians 1 that church members are responsible for ensuring that the teaching in their church is faithful to God's Word.

Since God's Word is all-important for Christian life and growth, and since we as church members are responsible for ensuring that God's Word is faithfully taught, we need to understand what good preaching is and how to benefit from good preaching. These aren't just topics for seminary students. Every Christian has an eternal interest in good preaching.

In this study, we want to think specifically about the point of preaching and the related question, what makes a good sermon good?

MAIN IDEA

God's people need to hear from God. Therefore, good preaching is preaching that places its highest priority on faithfully communicating God's Word.

DIGGING IN

Let's begin near the beginning by thinking about what went wrong in the world and why fallen humanity is in the condition it's in.

In Genesis 2, God told Adam and Eve, "You may surely eat of every tree of the garden, but of the tree of the knowledge of good and evil you shall not eat" (vv. 16–17). Sadly, Adam and Eve disobeyed God.

Here's how God describes what went wrong: he said to Adam, "Because you have listened to the voice of your wife and have eaten of the tree of which I commanded you, 'You shall not eat of it,' cursed is the ground because of you" (Gen. 3:17).

1. How does God describe Adam's failure?

2. In discussing Genesis 3, we often focus on the sin of pride, or the sin of wanting to become like God, which are ways of characterizing a heart problem. But it's also important to see that these "heart failures" showed up in Adam as "ear failures." What then do we learn from this passage about sin generally? Using the language of this passage, how will the temptation to sin show up in our lives?

3. If we, as fallen humans, are continually tempted to set our desires on hearing from voices other than God's, what kind of preaching will we wrongly desire to hear?

4. As you sit and listen to sermons, what are some ways in which you personally show more interest in voices other than God's?

The apostle Paul was someone who knew well the importance of listening to God's Word as opposed to false teachers, humanly devised philosophies, or any other competitor. In one of the last letters of his life, he writes to his longtime disciple Timothy,

[16]All Scripture is breathed out by God and profitable for teaching, for reproof, for correction, and for training in righteousness, [17] that the man of God may be complete, equipped for every good work. [4:1] I charge you in the presence of God and of Christ Jesus, who is to

judge the living and the dead, and by his appearing and his kingdom: [2] preach the word; be ready in season and out of season; reprove, rebuke, and exhort, with complete patience and teaching. [3] For the time is coming when people will not endure sound teaching, but having itching ears they will accumulate for themselves teachers to suit their own passions, [4] and will turn away from listening to the truth and wander off into myths. (2 Tim. 3:16–4:4)

5. According to verse 16 of chapter 3, where does the Bible come from? Why should this cause us to believe and obey everything it says?

6. According to verses 16 and 17 of chapter 3, what will the Bible do for Christians?

7. In light of these two verses, how would you characterize the point of preaching? How would you answer the question, "What makes a good sermon good?"

8. Read 4:1. Paul starts with the words, "I charge you. . . . " By what or by whom does Paul charge Timothy? What does this say about how serious Paul is about what he's about to say? (Keep in mind that Paul is probably nearing his death and sitting in his prison cell as he writes to Timothy.)

9. Here at the end of his life, what is Paul most anxious to charge Timothy to do (4:2)?

10. What exactly is it that Timothy must preach (4:2)? What else might Timothy be tempted to preach?

Because God's people need to hear from God, and because God charges preachers to preach his Word, preachers should realize they have nothing truly valuable to say other than what's in God's Word. That's the job—to faithfully say again what God has already said in his Word; to explain it and apply it to the congregation so that, by the power of the Spirit, their lives will be conformed to God's will.

What makes a good sermon good? A good sermon is one that faithfully proclaims and applies the meaning of God's Word.

11. What might distract Timothy—or any pastor—from fulfilling this charge? What do you think Paul means by "in season and out of season" (4:2)?

12. How do verses 3 and 4 in chapter 4 remind you of our meditation on Genesis 2 and 3?

13. Should good preaching be measured by its outcome or its content?

14. What should churches be looking for in their preachers? What should you look for in a preacher when you are choosing a church?

WEEK 4
HOW DOES EXPOSITIONAL PREACHING WORK?

GETTING STARTED

1. How would you characterize the best preaching you've heard? What made it so good?

2. How would you characterize the worst *preaching you've heard? What made it so bad?*

In this study we're going to think a little more deeply about expositional preaching: what it is, how it works, and why pastors should mainly preach expositional series of sermons.

What Is Expositional Preaching?
As a refresher, here's what we mean by expositional preaching: preaching that takes the main point of a passage, makes that the main point of the sermon, and applies it to life today. Further, expositional preaching typically works through whole books of the Bible over time.

Other Options
Expositional preaching is by no means the only kind of preaching that's out there, nor even the most popular. In fact, there are a number of other methods of preaching that church leaders advocate and practice:

1. **Topical preaching.** The preacher selects a topic that is relevant and important to his hearers, gathers scriptural teaching on the subject, and delivers a practical, accessible message.

2. **Narrative preaching.** This can take the form of a biography of a biblical character or a notable Christian. A more popular form of narrative preaching is to tell a personal story or testimony that illustrates a spiritual point. If a narrative preacher is focusing on a text of Scripture, he makes sure to communicate it in the form of a story.
3. **"Progressive dialogue."** Some people claim that in this postmodern age, no one can bear to listen to one-sided, authoritarian monologues known as "sermons." So, they say, church leaders should engage in a kind of open-ended dialogue that equally embraces all viewpoints.

While the first two of these can certainly be helpful ways for pastors to preach occasionally, we're convinced that expositional preaching should be a church's main diet. Week in, week out, a pastor should normally preach expositional series of sermons.

Because expositional preaching is so important to the life of the church, we're going to spend this study examining the workings of and rationale for expositional preaching a little more deeply. We're going to see how expositional preaching *works*.

MAIN IDEA

In expositional preaching, the value of the whole Bible drives the week-to-week preaching agenda, and the point of each passage determines the point of each sermon.

DIGGING IN

In the previous study, we considered 2 Timothy 3:16–4:4. To begin this study, we're going to briefly look again at 2 Timothy 3:16–17 from a slightly different angle.

After reminding Timothy that he had known the Scriptures from his youth and that the Scriptures are "able to make you wise for salvation through faith in Christ Jesus," Paul writes,

> [16] All Scripture is breathed out by God and is profitable for teaching, for reproof, for correction, and for training in righteousness, [17] that the man of God may be complete, equipped for every good work. (2 Tim. 3:16–17)

1. According to Paul, how much of Scripture is breathed out by God?

2. According to Paul, how much of Scripture is profitable for teaching, reproof, correction, and training in righteousness?

3. If all Scripture is profitable, we should be able to find good things in each of its parts. What are some things we uniquely learn from:

   a) The five books of Moses (Genesis, Exodus, Leviticus, Numbers, Deuteronomy)?

   b) The historical books of the Old Testament (Joshua through 2 Chronicles)?

   c) The Psalms?

   d) The Gospels?

   e) The New Testament Epistles?

4. Again, if all Scripture is profitable, which of the following do you think is a better week-to-week preaching agenda?

- The pastor picks a series of topics and finds Scriptures that discuss them.

- The pastor sets out to preach through books of the Bible.

How does expositional preaching work? Expositional preaching begins when the pastor decides to allow God to set the agenda rather than setting it himself. In expositional preaching, the value of the whole Bible drives the week-to-week preaching agenda. The conviction that all Scripture is profitable for teaching, rebuking, correcting, and training in righteousness leads the pastor to let books of the Bible set his agenda. And over time he aims to bring more of the riches of every part of God's Word to bear on his people's lives.

5. How will allowing Scripture itself to determine the preaching agenda help a pastor avoid the following common preaching pitfalls:

   a) Riding hobby horses?

   b) Avoiding the hard parts?

   c) Spiritually stagnating?

In Nehemiah 8 we see a real-life example of expositional preaching:

> [1] And all the people gathered as one man into the square before the Water Gate. And they told Ezra the scribe to bring the Book of the Law of Moses that the LORD had commanded Israel. [2] So Ezra the priest brought the Law before the assembly, both men and women and all who could understand what they heard, on the first day of the seventh month. [3] And he read from it facing the square before the Water Gate from early morning until midday, in the presence of the men and the women and those who could understand. And the ears of all the people were attentive to the Book of the Law. . . . [7] Also Jeshua, Bani, Sherebiah, Jamin, Akkub, Shabbethai, Hodiah, Maaseiah, Kelita, Azariah, Jozabad, Hanan, Pelaiah, the Levites, helped the people to understand the Law, while the people remained in their places. [8] They read from the book, from the Law of God, clearly, and they gave the sense, so that the people understood the reading. (8:1–3, 7–8)

While their context is certainly different from a Christian assembly, the basic idea is the same. Ezra and the Levites read the law and explained what it meant. Likewise, pastors who preach expositionally read a passage, explain it, and apply it.

How Does Expositional Preaching Work?
Just to recap, here are our two main ideas about how expositional preaching works:

1. the value of the whole Bible drives the week-to-week preaching agenda, and
2. the point of the passage determines the point of the sermon.

The "Why" of Expositional Preaching
For the remainder of our study, we're going to look at a passage of Scripture that gives us not the *how* of expositional preaching, but the *why*.

In Isaiah 55:10–11 God says,

> [10] For as the rain and the snow come down from heaven
>   and do not return there but water the earth,

making it bring forth and sprout,
  giving seed to the sower and bread to the eater,
[11] so shall my word be that goes out from my mouth;
  it shall not return to me empty,
but it shall accomplish that which I purpose,
  and shall succeed in the thing for which I sent it.

6. *To what does God compare his Word in this passage?*

7. *What do the "rain and snow" that "come down from heaven" do (v. 10)?*

8. *In verse 11, what does God say his Word won't do? What does God say his Word will do?*

9. *In light of this passage, how would you describe or characterize God's Word? According to this passage, why should pastors preach expositionally?*

10. *In light of the truth that God works by his Word, evaluate the other methods of preaching we discussed at the beginning of the study:*

  a) "Progressive dialogue"
  b) Topical preaching
  c) Narrative preaching

11. *In this passage God teaches us to trust wholeheartedly in the power of his Word. What might that trust look like in the following situations:*

  a) An evangelistic conversation you have with a friend or neighbor?
  b) A parent disciplining an exasperating child?
  c) A pastor preaching on Sunday morning?

WEEK 5
HOW THE WORD SHOULD
FILL THE CHURCH'S
GATHERINGS

GETTING STARTED

1. *What makes a Christian worship service different from other kinds of public gatherings, such as:*

- A political rally?
- A rock concert?
- A sports event?

Whatever a church's weekly gatherings may or may not have in common with these other public gatherings, one of the things that should set them apart the most is the pervasive presence of the Word of God.

As we saw in the previous study, pastors should preach expositionally because the whole Bible is profitable for Christians and because God's Word is powerful to accomplish his purposes. Building on this theme, in this study we're going to consider how God's Word should fill every aspect of the church's weekly gatherings. This sends us a bit downstream from preaching, but we're still considering the power of God's Word and its role in the life of the church.

MAIN IDEA

Every element of a church's weekly gatherings should be filled with God's Word. Through them the Word of Christ dwells in the church richly, building it up.

DIGGING IN

In Colossians 3, Paul sets out some of the corporate dimensions of how we are to live in light of the gospel. He writes,

> [12] Put on then, as God's chosen ones, holy and beloved, compassionate hearts, kindness, humility, meekness, and patience, [13] bearing with one another and, if one has a complaint against another, forgiving each other; as the Lord has forgiven you, so you also must forgive. [14] And above all these put on love, which binds everything together in perfect harmony. [15] And let the peace of Christ rule in your hearts, to which indeed you were called in one body. And be thankful. [16] Let the word of Christ dwell in you richly, teaching and admonishing one another in all wisdom, singing psalms and hymns and spiritual songs, with thankfulness in your hearts to God. [17] And whatever you do, in word or deed, do everything in the name of the Lord Jesus, giving thanks to God the Father through him. (3:12–17)

Note: In this study we're going to focus especially on verse 16.

1. Who is Paul addressing in these verses? (Hint: The "you" in verse 16 is plural in the Greek.)

2. What does it mean for the Word of Christ to dwell in the church richly (v. 16)?

3. What does the language of "dwelling richly" teach us about the Word of Christ itself? (Hint: Read Hebrews 4:12–13 and Isaiah 55:10–11 for background.)

4. By means of what specific activities does Paul instruct the Colossians to let the Word of Christ dwell in them richly?

5. What's the most obvious context in which Paul's instructions in verse 16 should be carried out? Explain.

6. What are different ways that Christians teach and admonish one another in their corporate gatherings, as described in this passage and the rest of the New Testament?

Ligon Duncan summarizes the New Testament teaching about what activities church gatherings should include in a way that sounds a lot like Colossians 3:16. He says that churches should:

- Read the Bible (1 Tim. 4:13)
- Preach the Bible (2 Tim. 4:2)
- Pray the Bible (1 Tim. 2:8)
- Sing the Bible (Col. 3:16)
- "See" the Bible, in the "visible words" of baptism and the Lord's Supper (Matt. 28:19; 1 Cor. 11:17–34)

This summary is helpful for a couple reasons. First, it summarizes what the New Testament instructs Christians to do in their corporate gatherings. Second, it shows how, through all of those elements, the Word of Christ is to dwell richly in the church's corporate assembly.

7. *Prayer is one way that Christians not only lift up their hearts to God but also instruct each other. With that in mind, how can those who lead the church in praying ensure that the Word of Christ is building up the church through their prayers?*

8. *How is it that the Word of Christ can dwell in us richly through singing "psalms and hymns and spiritual songs"? What does this require of the songs that we sing?*

9. *By what criteria would the apostle Paul evaluate the music he encountered in church? How does this differ from how we often evaluate music in church?*

10. *Based on Paul's teaching in verse 16, what are the purposes for which Christians should gather? What should we aim to do when we come together as a church?*

11. *What are some examples of things that may occur in a church's worship service that, rather than build up the church through the Word, actually distract the church from that goal?*

We've seen in previous studies that God's Word is powerful to accomplish his purposes and transform our lives. Therefore, pastors should preach sermons that take the main point of a passage of Scripture and make it the main point of the sermon.

And, as we've seen from Colossians 3 in this study, Paul also teaches us to make the Word of God central to everything we do as a gathered church. God's Word should always be on our lips as we sing, admonish one another, and pray.

12. What are some practical ways you can strive to let the Word of God dwell in you richly:

a) When you gather with the church on Sundays?

b) In your interactions with fellow church members during the week?

WEEK 6
PREACHING IS NOT
THE ONLY MINISTRY
OF THE WORD

GETTING STARTED

This whole study has been devoted to expositional preaching. As we've seen, it should be at the very center of the church's life. Yet preaching is definitely *not* the only ministry of the Word. In this final study we're going to consider how all Christians are called to minister the Word to each other.

1. What are some examples of "one-on-one ministry of the Word"? How do they differ from preaching?

MAIN IDEA

The New Testament calls all Christians to speak the Word to each other in order to help each other grow to maturity in Christ.

DIGGING IN

Acts 18 contains one of the more endearing scenes in the earliest history of the church. Luke writes,

> [24] Now a Jew named Apollos, a native of Alexandria, came to Ephesus. He was an eloquent man, competent in the Scriptures. [25] He had been instructed in the way of the Lord. And being fervent in spirit, he spoke and taught accurately the things concerning Jesus, though he knew only the baptism of John. [26] He began to speak boldly in the synagogue, but when Priscilla and Aquila heard him, they took him aside and explained to him the way of God more accurately. [27] And when he wished to cross to Achaia, the brothers encouraged him and

wrote to the disciples to welcome him. When he arrived, he greatly helped those who through grace had believed, [28] for he powerfully refuted the Jews in public, showing by the Scriptures that the Christ was Jesus. (18:24–28)

1. What did Priscilla and Aquila do for Apollos?

2. Were Priscilla and Aquila pastors or other specially appointed church leaders?

In 2 Timothy 1:5, Paul writes about another kind of one-to-one ministry of the Word:

[5] I am reminded of your sincere faith, a faith that dwelt first in your grandmother Lois and your mother Eunice and now, I am sure, dwells in you as well.

Then in 2 Timothy 3:14–15 Paul reminds Timothy,

[14] But as for you, continue in what you have learned and have firmly believed, knowing from whom you learned it [15] and how from childhood you have been acquainted with the sacred writings, which are able to make you wise for salvation through faith in Christ Jesus.

3. In view of these two passages, who do you think taught Timothy the Scriptures in his childhood?

4. Based on the passages we've just examined in Acts and 2 Timothy, would it be fair to say that the pastors were the only ones who taught the Word in the earliest days of Christianity? Why or why not?

In Colossians 3:16, which we also examined in our previous study, Paul writes,

Let the word of Christ dwell in you richly, teaching and admonishing one another in all wisdom, singing psalms and hymns and spiritual songs, with thankfulness in your hearts to God.

5. According to Paul, who in the church is supposed to teach and admonish others? (Hint: In the original Greek, the "you" in verse 16 is plural.)

6. Do you typically think of teaching and admonishing as exclusively the pastor's job or as the responsibility of every church member?

In Ephesians 4, Paul explains that pastors are to equip the saints for the work of ministry so that the whole church would be built up to maturity in Christ and would not be blown and tossed by every wind of doctrine:

> [15] Rather, speaking the truth in love, we are to grow up in every way into him who is the head, into Christ, [16] from whom the whole body, joined and held together by every joint with which it is equipped, when each part is working properly, makes the body grow so that it builds itself up in love. (vv. 15–16)

7. According to verses 15–16, by what means does the body of Christ grow to maturity?

8. How many of the body's members contribute to its growth by speaking the truth in love?

These two passages explicitly teach what we see modeled in Acts 18 and in 2 Timothy: all Christians are to speak the truth in love to one another to help the whole body grow to maturity in Christ. In Colossians 3:16, Paul describes this in terms of the Word dwelling in the church richly. In Ephesians 4:15–16, we see that we are to speak the truth in love so that we are no longer tossed to and fro by every wave of doctrine.

What does this mean in practical terms? It means that all Christians, not just pastors and other recognized teachers, should teach other believers the Word of God and help them apply it to their lives. This may take place most frequently in one-on-one or small-group settings rather than in public ministry such as preaching or Sunday-school teaching. But the diversity of settings only contributes to the richness of the church's overall ministry of the Word.

9. How will a lack of vibrant expositional preaching from the pulpit hinder one-on-one ministry of the Word in the lives of members? How will a rich diet of expositional preaching enable and inform one-on-one ministry of the Word?

10. How have you benefitted from other Christians personally teaching you the Word of God?

11. What are some specific ways in which you could work this kind of personal ministry of the Word into the existing routines and rhythms of your life?

TEACHER'S NOTES FOR WEEK 1

DIGGING IN

1. The two halves of this Psalm (vv. 1–6 and 7–11) teach that God reveals himself in creation and in his Word, in nature and in Scripture.

2. From God's revelation of himself in creation we learn of God's glory (v. 1), his wisdom (as seen in "his handiwork," v. 1), his beauty, and his power.

3. Creation can't teach us about:

- The multifaceted richness of God's moral character (although God has stamped a sense of his moral character upon all men's consciences)
- How sinful people can be reconciled to a holy God

4. All of these terms refer to God's Word. While some of them apply more directly to specific portions of God's Word, all of them can refer more broadly to God's Word as a whole. This array of terms teaches us that God speaks to us in Scripture in a rich variety of ways, all of which build us up in the true knowledge of God and conform us more closely to his character.

5. According to verses 7 through 11, God's Word:

- Revives the soul (v. 7)
- Makes the simple wise (v. 7)
- Causes the heart to rejoice (v. 8)
- Enlightens the eyes, that is, gives understanding and wisdom (v. 8)
- Warns God's servants (v. 11)

The human needs and situations God's Word addresses are (in order):

- Our need for spiritual life, encouragement, and refreshment
- Our ignorance and need for wisdom
- Sadness or heaviness of heart
- Ignorance and need for understanding and discernment
- Our sinful tendency to stray from God's ways

8. What's wrong with the churches in Galatia is that false teachers have preached a false gospel, and the churches have begun to believe it! Who is responsible? Both the false teachers and every single member who has allowed them to spread this false teaching in their church.

9. Based on Paul's teaching in this passage, both the church's leaders (whom the Bible calls "elders" or "pastors") *and* the congregation as a whole are responsible to ensure that the gospel is faithfully proclaimed in the church.

10. The danger of congregations totally entrusting this responsibility to their leaders is that if the leaders begin to stray doctrinally, the church won't have the discernment or the practical mechanism necessary for correcting or silencing those who teach false doctrine. Another danger is that, in handing over doctrinal responsibility entirely to the leadership, the church will fail to grow in doctrinal discernment and maturity as they ought to.

11. For the average church member, this responsibility looks like

- Regularly growing in the knowledge of God's Word
- Praying for the faithfulness of those who teach
- Encouraging and investing in the training of future pastors and elders
- Humbly asking questions when you don't understand something or when it seems as though a teacher has said something out of accord with God's Word
- When necessary, working together with the whole church to correct those teachers who are in significant error

12. Telling a pastor what to preach and appointing review committees would be extreme, unwarranted applications of this passage that miss the point. How then can churches rightly exercise this responsibility while still submitting to their leaders? The key is humility. Churches should cultivate a posture of submission, respect, and trust for their leaders while simultaneously encouraging every church member to search the Scriptures and carefully weigh what is taught (Acts 17:11). One thing that will significantly help in this regard is if leaders demonstrably cultivate humility and invite the congregation's feedback and questions.

13. Answers will vary.

TEACHER'S NOTES FOR WEEK 3

GETTING STARTED

1. The purpose of listening to sermons is to hear from God. It's to learn about who he is, who we are as individuals and as a people, and what he intends for our lives.

2. The purpose is not to be entertained. It's not to learn about the personal life of the pastor or what his opinions are on any number of topics. It's not to be challenged by some system of human philosophy or reasoning. The purpose is to hear from God.

DIGGING IN

1. In this passage God describes Adam's failure as not listening to God's voice and listening instead to another voice that led him astray from what God said.

2. In general, sin can be characterized as listening to voices other than God's. Temptation shows up in the form of these other voices, calling us to do something contrary to God's Word.

3. We will be tempted to want to hear anything *other* than faithful exposition of the Scriptures. We'll want to hear jokes, personal stories, interesting historical facts, and so forth. Some of these things are not bad in themselves, and they can certainly be used to good effect in preaching. But we need to be careful that we don't grow more interested in them than in a preacher's explanation of and exhortation from the biblical text. Even more dangerous, of course, is our desire to hear unbiblical doctrine or preaching that allows us to cherish our sins rather than put them to death. Our hearts will sinfully want the preacher to downplay the more difficult truths of Christianity, or to not preach about them at all.

4. Answers will vary.

5. Second Timothy 3:16 tells us that the Bible comes from God. It is inspired by him, literally "breathed out" by him. It is his Word.

6. Second Timothy 3:16–17 teaches that the Bible teaches us, reproves us, corrects us, and trains us in righteousness. It makes us competent disciples of Christ so that we are ready to live lives characterized by every good work.

7. The point of preaching is to teach, reprove, correct, and train a congregation through the Word of God. It's to equip a congregation for good works. A good sermon is good because it faithfully transmits what God says, like a mailman who simply delivers the mail.

8. Paul charges Timothy "in the presence of God," and by "Christ Jesus, who is to judge the living and the dead," and by Christ's kingdom and appearing. This list tells us that Paul is as serious as he could possibly be about what he is about to say. Paul is speaking of the most eternally weighty realities imaginable.

9. Paul is most anxious to charge Timothy to faithfully preach God's Word, that is, the Scripture that God inspired, which centers on the good news of salvation through Jesus Christ.

10. Timothy must preach *the Word*, that is, God's Word, God's message. Timothy may be tempted to preach his opinions, his personality and his life experiences, or worldly philosophies and opinions. Why? Because the world (and even some within the church!) will oppose God's Word. God's Word unmasks our sin and calls us to repent of it, and we sinners will devise all means possible in order to avoid that divine confrontation.

11. Any number of things may distract Timothy from this charge: his frequent illnesses (1 Tim. 5:23), false teachers who contradict his message, opposition within the church, desire for riches or prominence, and much more. By "in season and out of season" (4:2) Paul means that, when it's easy or when it's hard, he should preach. When the people want it or don't want it, he should preach. When he's popular, when he's not popular, he should preach the Word.

12. These verses present an "inside the church" example of how church members will want to hear voices other than God's, just as Adam chose to listen to his wife rather than to listen to God.

13. Preaching should be measured principally by its content, not by its delivery or by the outcome of that preaching. Just because people flock to hear a charismatic preacher doesn't mean he's a good or successful preacher. The successful preacher, in God's eyes, is the preacher who is faithful to God's Word. Period. As Paul puts it, "I planted, Apollos watered, but God gave the growth" (1 Cor. 3:6). Good preaching scatters seed. That's it. God determines the outcome.

14. What should churches (and individual Christians) look for in a pastor?

- Faithfulness to God's Word
- Dedication to God's Word

- A deep and abiding love for God's Word, as evidenced in his words and actions, in his home and in his public life
- More than anything, what makes a good pastor is that he faithfully preaches and lives out God's Word

TEACHER'S NOTES FOR WEEK 4

DIGGING IN

1. According to Paul, *all* of Scripture is breathed out by God (v. 16).

2. According to Paul, *all* of Scripture is profitable for teaching, reproof, correction, and training in righteousness (v. 16).

3. There are dozens of valid answers. Here's just a sampling of what we uniquely learn from these different portions of Scripture:

a) The five books of Moses: 1) God's creation of the whole universe; 2) God redeeming Israel out of Egypt; 3) God's holiness as revealed in his law.

b) The historical books of the Old Testament: 1) The people of Israel's constant slide into sin; 2) The depth, and limits, of God's patience.

c) The Psalms: how to personally relate to, depend on, worship, and pray to God.

d) The Gospels: the life, teaching, death, and resurrection of Jesus.

e) The New Testament Epistles: how to live as Christians, in the church, in light of the gospel.

4. While this question is asking for a personal assessment and opinion, the answer we *hope* the class will arrive at is the second one: that it is better for a pastor to set out to preach through books of the Bible. Why? Because preaching through Scripture recognizes the value of the whole Bible for transforming God's people. It shows that a pastor is determined to let God set the agenda for the church.

5. Here are some ways that expositional preaching helps a pastor avoid the following common pitfalls:

a) Expositional preaching will keep a pastor from **riding hobby horses** because it will force him to address what arises in the text of Scripture rather than simply the topics he wants to address.

b) Expositional preaching will keep a pastor from **avoiding the hard parts of Scripture** because he is committing to communicating exactly what God says as he works through a book passage-by-passage. If a pastor is really preaching expositionally, he can't simply skip a passage that contains something he'd rather not address.

c) Expositional preaching helps a pastor not **stagnate spiritually** because it forces him to wrestle with the Word of God week-after-week. If a pastor preaches topically, he can simply teach from his existing knowledge of Scripture. By preaching expositionally, however, he is forced to face new texts week-after-week, which challenges and grows him in the knowledge of Scripture. This should have a refreshing and energizing effect on the pastor's soul.

6. In this passage, God compares his Word to the rain and snow that come down from heaven and water the earth.

7. According to verse 10, the rain and snow water the earth, cause it to grow plants and thereby supply seed for sowing and bread for food.

8. In verse 11, God says that his Word *won't return to him empty*, but that it *will accomplish* all of his purpose and *will succeed* in the thing for which he sent it.

9. In light of this passage we could characterize God's Word as effective, powerful, active, effectual, unstoppable, unfailing, and more. Pastors should preach expositionally because God works by his Word. Because God's Word is powerful, effectual, and unstoppable. Because God's Word will accomplish all his purposes.

10. a) "Progressive dialogue" falls short of reflecting the truth of this passage because it refuses to submit to the authority of God's Word. If all voices are to be equally respected in the church, then men have taken the place of God.

b) Topical preaching may have good uses from time to time, but a regular diet of topical preaching typically means the pastor will fail to fully expound what God has said. God didn't choose to inspire just verses or passages; he chose to inspire whole books, which consist of whole literary sections and paragraphs. Thus, the way to fully harness the power of God's Word is to preach *what he has said*. This requires a preacher to take the main point of a passage and make that the main point of the sermon, rather than consistently starting with a topic already in mind and using Scripture to support it.

c) Narrative preaching falls short in that it either relegates Scripture to a secondary role in the sermon or attempts to force all of Scripture into a narrative mold. In either case, it generally shares the weaknesses of topical preaching.

11. Answers will vary.

TEACHER'S NOTES FOR WEEK 5

DIGGING IN

1. Paul is addressing the whole church at Colossae.

2. The Word dwelling richly in the church means that it echoes through the church, reverberates through the life of the church, works its way into individuals' lives and relationships, and causes the church to grow in maturity in Christ. The root word for dwell means "house." It's as if the Word should make its home in the life of the congregation.

3. The language of "dwelling richly" indicates that Christ's Word is living and active, that it's powerful and effectual (see Isa. 55:10–11; Heb. 4:12–13).

4. Paul exhorts the Colossians to let the Word of Christ dwell richly in them by teaching and admonishing one another, and by singing psalms and hymns and spiritual songs.

5. The most obvious context in which Paul's instructions should be carried out is the assembly of the whole church. Paul is addressing the whole church, and his mention of singing suggests a corporate gathering of the whole church.

6. In their corporate gatherings, Christians teach and admonish one another by:

   a) Preaching (1 Tim. 4:13)
   b) Publicly reading Scripture (1 Tim. 4:13)
   c) Praying (1 Tim. 2:8)
   d) Singing (Col. 3:16)
   e) Stirring one another up with spiritually pointed conversation (Col. 3:16; Heb. 10:24–25)

7. Those who lead the church in prayer can strive to ensure that the Word of Christ builds up the church through their prayers by incorporating biblical petitions, biblical truths, and biblical models of relating to God in their public prayers. This doesn't necessarily mean that those who lead the church in prayer *must* prepare ahead of time. However, advance preparation is certainly a wise way for those who lead in prayer to serve the whole church by working to make their prayers thoroughly biblical.

8. The Word of Christ can dwell in the church through singing insofar as we sing songs that are filled with the Word of Christ. At the very least, this requires that the songs we sing are filled with biblical doctrine, phrases, concepts, and language. Put negatively, it also requires that our songs do not convey any unbiblical ideas. It also requires that the Word of God is not drowned out by the music that is supposed to support it. And, since Paul mentions singing psalms, it means that Christians should sing psalms and other portions of Scripture as well!

9. Paul would evaluate music he heard in church based on whether it caused the Word to dwell richly in the church. That is, he would primarily evaluate the music based on its scriptural content. This differs from us in that we so often evaluate music primarily in terms of whether it conforms to our stylistic preferences.

10. Based on verse 16, we could say that one of the primary goals of Christians assembling together is to build one another up through the Word of Christ, as well as to offer worship to God (cf. v. 16, "with thankfulness in your hearts *to God*"). When we come together as a church, we should aim to build up the whole church body through teaching, admonishing, singing, and other activities through which the Word dwells in us richly.

11. Answers will vary. One way to look at this question is that anything that seeks to entertain people more than edify them can distract the church from the goal of building each other up by the Word. Examples of this are too numerous to count!

12. Answers will vary.

TEACHER'S NOTES FOR WEEK 6

DIGGING IN

General suggestion: If you can, work through the first eight questions a little more quickly than normal so that you leave plenty of time to discuss the more application-oriented questions nine through eleven.

1. Priscilla and Aquila took Apollos aside and instructed him more accurately regarding the good news of what Christ had accomplished through his death and resurrection.

2. As far as we know from the biblical account, Priscilla and Aquila were simply "regular" Christians, not pastors or specially appointed teachers in a local church.

3. In view of these two passages in 2 Timothy, it seems likely that Timothy's mother and grandmother are the ones who taught him the Scriptures when he was a child.

4. Based on these passages in Acts and 2 Timothy, it would *not* be fair to say that in the earliest days of Christianity the only ones who taught the Word were pastors. Rather, while there were men who were specially set aside to preach and teach publicly (1 Tim. 5:17), it seems that all kinds of Christians taught the Word to each other.

5. According to Paul's teaching in Colossians 3:16, all Christians are supposed to teach and admonish the members of their local churches.

6. Answers will vary.

7. According to Ephesians 4:15–16, the body of Christ grows to maturity as all the members speak the truth in love to one another. This happens as each part (that is, each church member) is working properly and contributes to the body building itself up.

8. All of the body's members contribute to its growth through speaking the truth in love, as Paul's phrase, "when each part is working properly," indicates.

9. A lack of vibrant expositional preaching will hinder one-on-one ministry of the Word in the church in two ways. First, the congregation simply won't

be learning the Word the way they should from the preaching. Second, congregations will seldom take greater care with God's Word than what they see exampled in the pulpit. On the other hand, a steady diet of expositional preaching should fuel a slew of one-on-one ministry of the Word. When pastors preach expositionally, they model proper biblical interpretation and application, and they equip church members not only to learn the Bible but also to go and teach it to others.

10–11. Answers will vary.

PERSONAL NOTES

PERSONAL NOTES

PERSONAL NOTES

PERSONAL NOTES

PERSONAL NOTES

PERSONAL NOTES

IX 9Marks

Building Healthy Churches

9Marks exists to equip church leaders with a biblical vision and practical resources for displaying God's glory to the nations through healthy churches.

To that end, we want to see churches characterized by these nine marks of health:

1   Expositional Preaching
2   Biblical Theology
3   A Biblical Understanding of the Gospel
4   A Biblical Understanding of Conversion
5   A Biblical Understanding of Evangelism
6   Biblical Church Membership
7   Biblical Church Discipline
8   Biblical Discipleship
9   Biblical Church Leadership

Find all our Crossway titles
and other resources at
www.9Marks.org

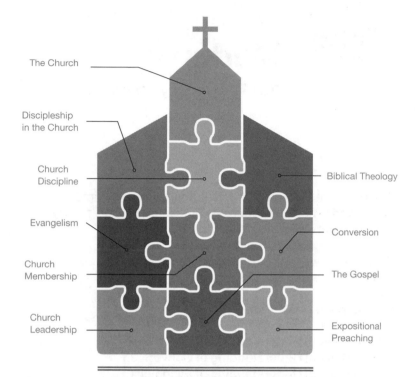

The Church

Discipleship
in the Church

Church
Discipline

Biblical Theology

Evangelism

Conversion

Church
Membership

The Gospel

Church
Leadership

Expositional
Preaching

Be sure to check out the rest of the
**9MARKS HEALTHY CHURCH
STUDY GUIDE SERIES**

This series covers the nine distinctives
of a healthy church as originally laid out
in *Nine Marks of a Healthy Church* by
Mark Dever. Each book explores the
biblical foundations of key aspects of
the church, helping Christians to live
out those realities as members of a
local body. A perfect resource for use in
Sunday school, church-wide studies, or
small group contexts.